Separating Beads

A Book of Poems

S. E. Thomas

Separating Beads
A Book of Poems

S. E. Thomas

Published by The Dramatic Pen Press, L.L.C.

Lolo, Montana

ISBN-10: 1-64157-009-1
ISBN-13: 978-1-64157-009-1

For my incredible husband, Aaron.

Thank you for being the answer to all the

desperate questions of my youth.

For my incredible husband, Aaron.

Thank you for being the answer to all the desperate questions of my youth.

Table of Contents

Author's Note

The poetry you will find here spans several seasons of my life. Some of the poems are from my point of view, and some are from the point of view of someone else. Some are romantic, some are serious, and some are humorous, but all of them represent a memory or an emotion that became part of the fabric of my life.

They are intended to inspire emotion, nostalgia or even curiosity, but not all are intended to teach. Some things must be said, merely because they are felt… not because they are true. And so, as you laugh, cry or remember, I hope you will enjoy my poetry and add to it something of yourself.

Susan Elizabeth Thomas

~ Theme Poem ~

Separating Beads

I'm separating beads,
Picking out all the dark blue ones.
They are everywhere.
I separate beads
Like I separate my feelings.
Dark mixed with the bright.
Emotions
Beads
Love
Despair
Loving again
Fear
Of losing again
Separating
Analyzing
Trying to understand
Why—
Why are there
So many colors
All mixed up.
I'll never be finished
Separating beads.

~ *Nature* ~

Romantic Rain

When the rain is falling down
it beats the dust into the ground
rebounding wildly off cement
dampening over the April scent
causing a humid mist to see
small rivers flowing merrily.
The earth calls out a lazy chant
and tempts my thirst for sweet romance.

Chaser

A limerick.

My cat is quite a good chaser.
The squirrels and mice like to race her.
But in a tight pinch,
If they lose an inch,
They suddenly find they must face her.

Waterfall

Dribble
Bubble
Gurgle—pop!
In the milling stream I drop.

Swirling
Twirling
Flowing free
Sliding past a hundred trees.

Swishing
Sloshing
Spinning by
Reaching but there's nothing nigh.

Churning
Crashing
Buried deep
Up I come for just a peep.

Splashing
Lurching
Blasting on
Faster, faster and I'm gone.

Booming
Slashing
Falling down
Then just silence… as I drown.

The Cat's Gift

I just now opened my front door
And saw before me on the floor
A gift from Cat of half a squirrel.
The sight of it near made me hurl.

The bottom half—I know not where.
But I found the tail still lying there
And a perfectly extracted thing
That looked just like a kidney bean.

I had to clean it up right quick
Before the kids and I got sick.
That cat! I thought, with some chagrin.
…But still… I guess we're loved by him.

~ Youth & Childhood ~

Raising Boys

Bruises, black eyes, broken bones,
Avoiding karate kicking zones,
Sending them out to the park,
Stepping on Legos in the dark,
Streakers running swiftly by,
Now he's a ninja, now he's a spy.
Body humor, goofy songs,
Patching jeans, righting wrongs,
Jars of spiders, moths and snakes,
But, no scorpions, for goodness sake!
Finding Hot Wheels in my shoes,
"How many more gloves can you lose?"
Chicken pox and football games,
Laughing often keeps me sane.
Sound effects, big, strong hugs,
Sticky kisses, slimy doorknobs.
They're flexing muscles, acting tough,
Scaling walls in the buff,
Chasing the cat, climbing trees,
Making swords of everything.
Science projects, bee-bee guns,
Bows and arrows, tons of fun!
Life is full of many joys
When you're raising little boys.

Becoming

A seed of doubt
Is planted deep
The rains of question
Downward seep

A sprout of wonder
Push upward still
A blush, a smile
The fragile will

Growth comes slowly
Learning so bold
Sun shining brightly
The first leaf unfolds

A strain and a task
Is well underway
Push for true beauty
Live for the day

A bud is forming
It's hard when you're shy
Never to give up
Never to die

A tender blossom
A brand new start
To God my soul
To God my heart

First Discoveries

A naked child
Played and cooed;
His age was
Two or three.
He ran along
The sandy shore
Like sunshine
On the breeze.

He spotted
Something
Burrow deep;
And curious
As he was,
He squatted
Like an Indian chief
And watched
A sand flea buzz.

Soon his interest
Lost its wax,
And a shell
Did take its place.
He picked it up
With chubby hands
And brought it
Near his face.

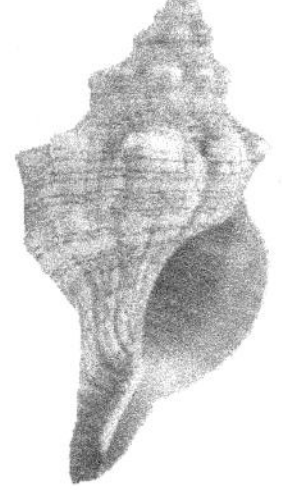

The sound of waves
Did catch
His ear

And amazed
Was he to find,
That trapped
Inside such small
A land
Was a sea
Of different kind.

Childhood Dreams

Once how I longed to fly,
To soar up high above the sky.
Then I wished to climb a tree
And drop down through our chimney.

I once wanted to be a fish
And swallow dimes that bought a wish.
I dreamed I was a princess fair
And wore gold ribbons in my hair.

I climbed a tree and imagined that
I was a pirate, mean and fat.
I built a fort and climbed inside,
Pretending that I had to hide.

I swung from one rope to another.
I was then a jungle-lover.
Now I'm older, or so I seem.
Yet I will never cease to dream.

Eighteen

The girl in me
Plays and pretends.
The woman in me
A willful dream tends.

The child I am
Wills to be free.
The woman I am
A wife longs to be.

Youth so alive!
Comfort with age?
In spirit I've yet
To come to this page.

Eager and quick,
Calm like a rose.
Failure and hardships—
Yet still the soul grows.

To be eighteen—
The time of choice.
I learn with my ears.
I teach with my voice.

Failure to Thrive

Shakespearean Sonnet

Listen to hear the beeps and breathing sounds.
The scent of medicine fills the air.
With doctors, nurses bustling around
How strange that they forget I am here.
The tubes are stretching far above my head.
My vision does not reach so far up high.
Each time I move I'm trapped upon my bed.
The tape and patches make me want to cry.
No one seems to care about my tears…
Can they not hear me each time I scream?
My body cramps and heaves as if in fear
Of something I am lacking—that I need.
Unless I'm touched and loved while I'm alive,
The time may come when I will fail to thrive.

My Little Newborn

You're my little newborn…
But how long will you be?
I wonder when you'll turn
Into a sweet baby?

And when you're my baby,
How long will it take,
For a toddler to grow
With the steps that you make?

And as a sweet toddler
(Who might drive me wild)
What ever will I do
When I find you're a child?

And I think of that child…
That I may just forbid
Ever to grow up
To become a kid.

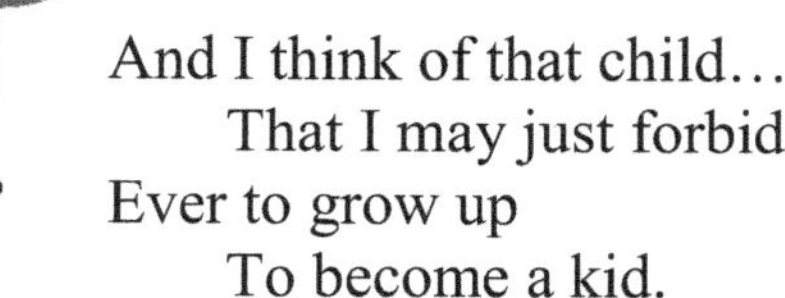

For perhaps that kid
Won't know what I mean,
When I say, "Oh, please,
Don't turn into a teen!"

And teenagers, I hear,
Can 'bout drive you mad!
…But there might come a day,
You'll become a dad.

And then when you visit,
I'm sure I'll adore
The moment you show me
Your little newborn.

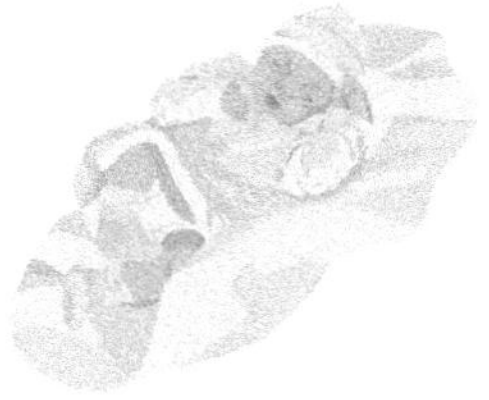

Kindred Spirits

My family took me to the ocean one day.
I saw a big whale swimming my way.

I said to my father, "Come look! Come see!
There's a giant whale coming towards me!"

But he only smiled and said to go swim.
I saw there was no use talking to him.

I went to my mother and told her the truth.
"The giant whale has a big golden tooth!"

She thought I was sick and made me lie down.
She said, "We'll see the doc when we get to town."

I went to my sister to tell her my tale.
But she was playing with the golden toothed whale.

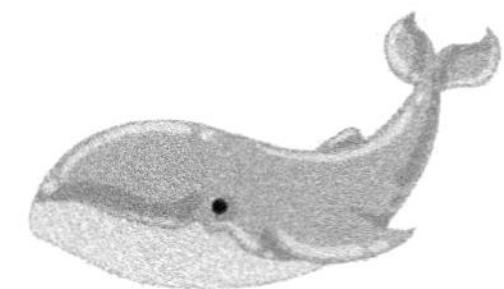

Careless

Once when I was
Far too young,
I kissed a man
I did not love.

He took my hand.
I played the part.
And then, at last,
I broke his heart.

A prideful sin
And willful game.
Then why do I
Not feel the shame?

~ Self-Doubt ~

The Sparrow

From my window
I now can see
a small sparrow
chuckling at me.
He never turns
His head around.
He winks at earth,
at sky, at ground.
He still pretends
to see me not.
A tear of ice.
Beauty forgot.
I know his thoughts.
They seem so kind.
He flies away;
leaves me behind.

Taking the Chance

I walked along a narrow path
and saw yonder my goal,
a wooden bridge that stretched across
a silver stream of old.

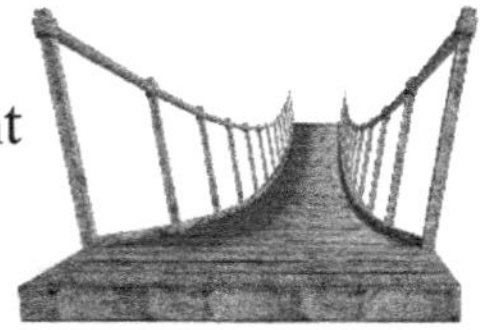

I blinked my eyes as morning light
met me from 'neath the trees.
I stood along the bank a bit
And felt the rustling breeze.

My hand reached out and touched the rail,
long since had been worn soft.
I contemplated at the brink,
this aged wood, still aloft.

How many had come through this place,
and on this bridge confide?
How many chanced to step across
to reach the other side?

Ancient temptation sapped my trust,
but could I stand and wait
until another came this way
to take the last safe gate?

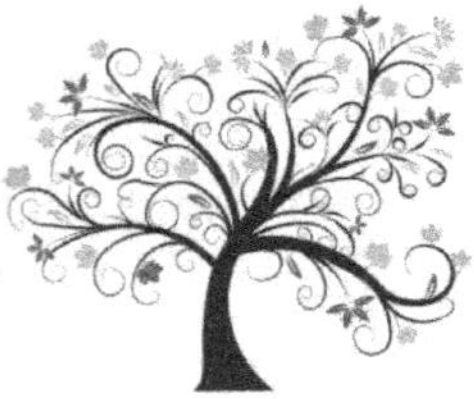

And so I took a trembling step
with hand upon the rail.
I crossed into the open space—
but paused at middle trail.

I was astonished by the sight
that chanced to meet my eyes.
The sunrise—a velvet masterpiece,
that God set in the skies.

I stood breathless—left in pure awe;
Such beauty had been shown.
But if I hadn't crossed the bridge,
I would have never known.

Smoke and Fog

A fire caught in my home
and burned for ten years.
I got used to seeing
through the smoke.
Then someone came
to release me.
He opened the door.
I expected to see
the sunlight—
but, as I stepped
through the door,
I stepped into
a world
of fog.

Pray For Me

Won't you please forgive me
If I'm walking in confusion,
But my life up till now
Has been a massive delusion.

Pray for me…
To be free.

I cannot deny it;
I have made some awful choices.
How can I find the truth
Through so many other voices?

Pray for me…
To be free.

I see only friends now,
And though this whole town is empty,
I can't shake the feeling
That there's someone out to get me.

Pray for me…
To be free.

Window

I am a window.
I break easily.
Sometimes people hurl stones at me
with words they say…
without realizing what they are doing…
I am hard to see.
You must look closely.
When you look through me and see me not,
it hurts.
Little pieces
chip
and fall
to the ground.
Sometimes people step on the
bitter,
sharp
pieces when they walk too close.

They get cut
and when they see their blood
they realize
that someone had to break a part of me
before I could hurt anyone else.
I didn't do it on purpose.
I wanted someone to sweep up the pieces.
I don't know how.
When I saw you walking towards me
I was frightened.
What if you saw through me?
What if you stepped on the broken bits?
What if I saw you bleeding because of
me?

I was afraid for you.
I was afraid for me.
I tried to warn you.
I turned so that the sun
would shine brightly in your eyes.
Maybe you would turn away
and be safe.
I tried to warn you…
but I wanted you to come.
I secretly hoped you would see
me.

I hoped.
You stepped closer
and looked.
You looked for a long time.
No one had ever looked for so long.
I knew you were seeing me.
You thought I was pretty—
even though I was cracked and broken in places.
But you came too close
and now you're bleeding, too.
I'm so sorry.
I'm so, so sorry.
I have hurt the only one
I have ever loved…
And I don't know how to
make it better.

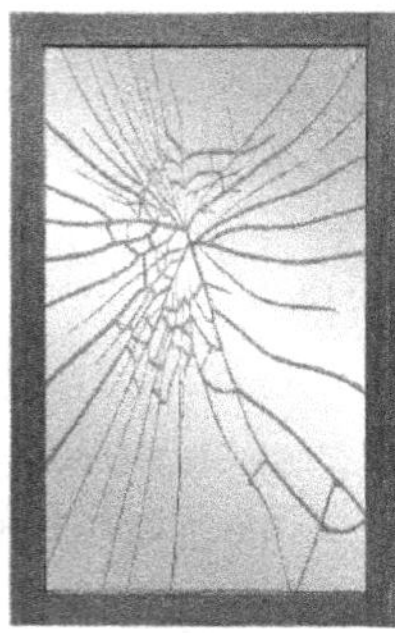

Losing Myself

I'm losing myself
in my surroundings
my attention
stolen
I'm losing myself
in people
in friends
if they are
I'm losing myself
in activity
in socialization
in work
without rest
I need time alone
I need to ignore
to be ignored
I need peace
time
to find what I lost
was it ever mine
I'm losing myself
I'm lost
I need to scream
and not be heard.

Confusion

Lost in a sea
of broken riddles
Floating by lee
of strangled thought
Trapped in a maze
of lost emotions
In heartless phase
my soul is caught

~ Beauty ~

Beauty

There is beauty captured in a rose
and in a baby's smile.
There is beauty in a traveler's song
as he roams, mile 'pon mile.

There is beauty in a rainy night
and in a whistled tune.
There is beauty in a bride's sweet kiss
and in a crescent moon.

There is beauty locked up in your eyes
and in a rooster's crow.
There is beauty in a child's laugh
and in the choice to grow.

There is beauty in a horse's grace
and in a stranger's nod.
There is beauty in your simple faith
and beauty comes from God.

Beauty in Song

Notes so light as a breath on the wind.
I fly as a kite, held tight by a friend.
A twinge of fear, a burst of glee
The song I hear—a soft melody
A graceful bow; the taste of love,
My voice endow to glide as a dove
I've learned to dream; I've learned to dance
My soul to redeem, my heart to romance.

The Rose

A rose bit me the other day.
I yipped and turned as if to say,
"Why did you bite? I trusted you!"
It looked at me and said, "Boo, hoo!"

I swung at it, but my hand slid;
Across its velvet petals skid.
And then it turned its head to me.
I fell in love with its beauty.

I wished that I could be its friend,
But as I reached, it bit again.

~ Betrayal ~

Waking

A whisper nudged and bade me close.
"Who is the one you dream of most?"

I could not say. I must not tell
For fear that I might break the spell.

The whisper nudged and breathed again,
"I'm not a dream—but your true friend."

You lie to me. I must conceal
This love that I so strongly feel.

"Then say it loud and play the part.
Today—right now—this dream must start."

I spoke of him. I took the risk.
I'll not forgive the whisper this.

Then I awoke, tears in my eyes.
Why did I trust his hateful lies?

Thus still alone I am today
And for another dream I pray.

The Narcissist

I'm sad to see you crying.
I wish I felt the same.
I wish I could feel anything.
I wish I never came.

I wish I could have loved you
The way that you love me.
I truly tried to make it work—
But my love's lost, you see.

I told you that I loved you—
And yes, I guess I lied,
But how I wished it to be true.
At least, I truly tried.

I know that you've been crying.
You're hurt, alone, upset;
But I know you'll forgive me,
I know you love me yet.

Cheater Moon

The sun goes down
The moon comes out
And dances with the night.
A cheater's time—
To love the dark;
To use another's light.

The sun returns
Each day to shine
With no tears in her eyes.
But night will come
Again, lone one,
To boast its selfish lies.

~ *Friendship* ~

True Friend

We both have learned some things
That the other will never know.
We both have seen some places
To which the other will never go.

In spite of all our differences,
In spite of divided pasts,
I know God's love in you and me,
For each other will always last.

Tears glisten in my own eyes
When I hear about your pain.
When I see the things that hurt you,
Inside, my heart is slain.

You've taught me about my own self.
You've shown me all my pride.
You've listened and you've guided;
And you never once have lied.

Your simple faith and patience;
The way you humbly pray.
A love for God like yours
I hope I'll gain someday.

I could never ever repay you
For the joy you've given me.
I pray to God, that for someone else,
Such a friend I'll be.

Needed

A child brought me to my senses
the day I came to mend your fences.
He casually happened to mention
that he knew of my intentions.
And when I stopped to fix your sink,
his comments made me stop to think.
He asked me why I kept on coming—
if only to fix your leaky plumbing?
Of course, there is another reason
why I bother every season
to sweep your rooftop free of leaves,
replace old shingles, mend the reaves,
fix the hinge on your cellar door,
remove the cobwebs, wax the floor,
trim old branches from your trees,
repair your car, spray for bees.
Yes, perhaps, it's something more—
it's not the money—that's for sure!
It might just be, in my old age,
that loneliness has been upstaged
by something sweet I can't quite name.
Perhaps, your smile is to blame.
And though your voice is dear, 'tis true,
there's something more I've seen in you—
a sort of kinship I have found
in no other lady here around.
No, it's not love, as lovers go...
Though, were I younger, I don't know.
But, you are kind and sweet and dear
and I find welcome when I'm here.
And now that you have lost so much—
your husband and his loving touch—

I've come to find that I am needed—
if only to see your garden's seeded
or to see your windows hold
in all the heat and out the cold.
And when your pantry's looking bare
I might find something to leave there.
So, to that child, I guess I'll say,
it's nice to be needed in your own way
and maybe when your son grows tall
he won't concern himself at all
why I spend so much time of mine
to clean your chimney and trim your vines.
'Cause, for every smile it brings from you,
it turns about and brings me two.

Trusting Art

Never before could I express
The way I felt inside.
But when I look into your eyes,
My feelings I can't hide.

You listen as my bitter tears
Roll across my face.
You never chide, but give advice
With love and simple grace.

Each time we speak it's easier
For me to share my heart.
And now I find that I can learn
To use this trusting art.

Unfinished Poems

To me each soul is a poem
Which isn't yet complete.
The first few lines are written
At the moment that we meet.

A handshake or a smile
When we are drawing near.
The first few words are spoken.
I'll know if you're sincere.

The lines are slowly written.
Personalities revealed.
I question and I wonder
At what is still concealed.

We become much closer.
Most secrets now are gone.
Yet as we grow together
The poetry goes on.

The poems never finish
Until the day we die.
Perhaps we'll start again one day—
New poems in the sky.

~ Grief & Sorrow ~

A Tear

A tear is falling
          down the page
breaking painted hearts.

A clown is crying
          on the page—
a sad and happy art.

Misery

I smile

I laugh

I play silly jokes

you would never know

you cannot tell

I cry

I sink

in the depths of my misery

as soon as I am

alone.

Happy or Sad?
A Haiku

A clown is crying.
Tears erase a painted smile.
Should I laugh or cry?

The Actress

Ah,...
I see her—
she is lovely,
so attractive and talented.
She dances,
floats,
glides,
in her perfect part,
happy,
proud,
confident.
All men love her.
Women find
competition hard.
She cares not.
She loves and is loved.
For her, love is perfect.
But, when her part calls
for tears.
She is just as convincing—
maybe more so...
One might suspect
her agony is real.

Grieving

I am a child
Whose kitten just died.
I am a seashell—
Empty inside.

I am a sail
Without any wind.
I am a path
That comes to an end.

I am grieving
The loss of a dream.
Some speak of love;
How simple it seems.

But I am a dreamer
Just coming awake,
And I am a lover
Who loved by mistake.

Tears

Tears come to the edge of my eyes.
They deceive me into believing
I will have release...
but then they disappear,
leaving me
more sorrowful and helpless
than before.

I Am Transparent

I am transparent
None can see
I am a teardrop
Lost at sea

I am not real
But still alive
None can see
The hurt inside

I am a presence
Yet unknown
I wish my heart
Would turn to stone

I am transparent
None can see
I am a teardrop
Lost at sea

Shattered Pond

A wrinkled tear
        A shattered pond
A place where nothing goes just right
A blessed dance
        That falls apart
A gentle crying in the night

I'm not alone
        With none around
It seems I always find your face
And then I cry
        —a desperate sound
To know you, too, are in this place

If you escape
        I will be lost
But then perhaps I'll always be
But if you stay
        Don't look around
Lest you should find you could love me

~ Growth & Overcoming ~

Careless Note

A careless note leapt sharp
and free. It swung across a
melody. It sprinted flat on
rung
and
bar,
and
coaxed
the
song
to go
too far.
It slid
along the G-clef lap, and
stole the dots from Base-clef chap.
Then he bounced them word to word—
the sound of which became absurd. Then
the Master, stern with love, poked him
from the great above. And he in turn,
with guilt and shame, climbed again
from whence he came. The song
went on—not one note wrong.
Our careful friend became
a song.

Breaking Out

Calling out through
        glassy tears.
Breaking past these
        troubled years.

Shattering the
        crystal lies.
Stepping o'er the
        love denied.

The cuts will never
        Hold me back,
But spurn to strength
        The hope I lack.

Courage heals the
        prick of doubt.
Joy rewards my
        breaking out.

Experience

A choice is a doorway
A decision is a step
A mistake is not a failure
but a chance to look in-depth.

To choose is to discover
To decide is to learn
Conquest over loss
is to experience earn.

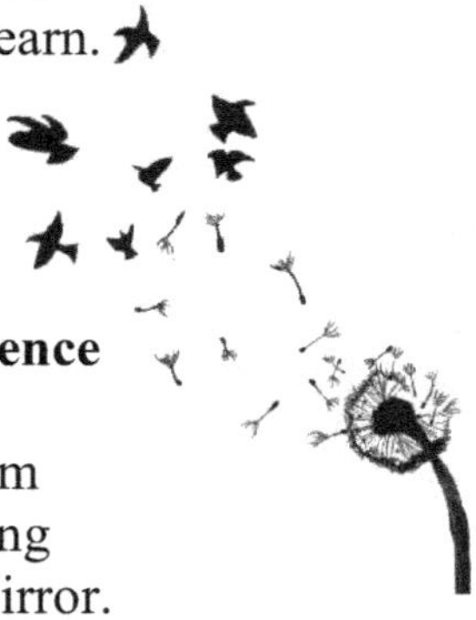

Transcendence

In a dream
I am falling
towards a mirror.
I can see myself
as I crash through.
But, it pops
like a bubble.
I am consumed by
darkness.
I am falling and falling....
or am I?
There is no light.
I realize
I am really flying
and I fly away
from everything.

Weeping Willow

I sat beneath a willow tree;
together we wept long.
I cried for her, she cried for me;
it was a mournful song.

Our tresses fell about our feet
as low we bent and cried.
At last my sorrows were quite spent,
but hers, she could not hide.

I tried to comfort her again
with new tears of my own;
but with each wind or gentle breeze
she wept a sigh or moan.

But then I chanced to leave her shade
and blew a kiss her way.
There was nothing I could do –
nothing I could say.

I heard her weeping as I left
but soon my tears had dried,
and once again I faced my fears
and once again I tried.

Now and then again we meet
I weep a tear or two.
But, I refuse to sit again –
for what good would it do?

in the turning

loving
        learning
bending backwards

caring
        earning
spending manners

falling
        seeing
past your wording

dreaming
        ending
in the turning

New Horizon

I see a new horizon.
I've found a new escape.
I'm glancing down new pathways.
My dreams are taking shape.

I'm looking only forward,
Though past—close by me still.
I pray that all my breathless hopes
Won't break my fragile will.

I've learned of pain and heartache
I know that love can lie
And so with wisdom laced with joy
I'll live, 'till last I die.

~ *Lost Love & Broken Relationships* ~

A Love Poem

Love, I am calling out your name,
Yet you do not respond.
My heart is searching for answers
To questions which haven't words.
Is it true that I must learn
To live my life without you?
Once my soul had been deceived.
True Love never dies.
True Love penetrates
Even the darkest hearts.
I will have the Love
That is promised me for all eternity.
It is sufficient for my soul;
It should be sufficient for my heart.
Yet, why am I still lonely
When I see lovers hand in hand?
Why do tears fall
Upon my solitary pillow?
I must learn to trust in Love.
He hears my desperate silent cries.
And He understands it all.

Compelled

From where I sit
I can see them rustling,
whispering,
asking me to come and look.
The lace curtains are beautiful,
as they glimmer and move
invitingly
in the bright sun.
But I am frightened.
I do not want to go
and see
what I already know is there.
But, I move anyway
forward
as one might play with a sore tooth
just to experience the pain
and feel it is real.
I look.
And I know my pain is real
as I gaze on the beautiful scene
of two lovers walking
hand in hand.

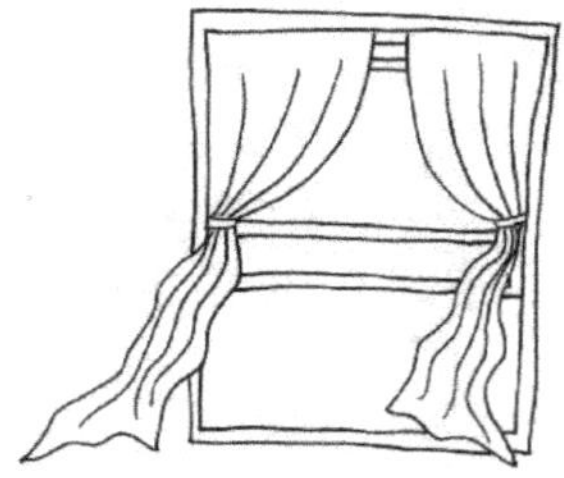

Blinded

I am blinded by my own self
In this love affair with you.
Learning to see beyond myself
Is very hard to do.

If I cannot love me with you,
I surely can't love you;
But in loving me, does it mean
The love we share is true?

I clearly see the man I am,
But you are hard to see;
And so I am ashamed at times
To find you loving me.

Losing You

Losing touch and losing sight
Losing more of you each night
Cradle fate within your arms
Battle 'gainst her fleeting charms

Where I once had rested sound
Now I'm swiftly losing ground
I will soon give up my fight
As I lose you night by night

Elusive

A Shakespearean Sonnet

Of roses and of springtime love is made
And lovers hand in hand along the walk
Where butterflies and cupids promenade,
When eyes will tell the story more than talk.
And this is what I see when sitting there,
The lovers floating like they're in a dream;
But in my life I find it is not fair
That love for me is not what it would seem.
But yet I wonder of the love of two
Wherever I can glimpse the hand of fate;
And wonder if for me it could be true
That one day I might find the perfect mate.
But if the past is what the future brings,
Then love is of the most elusive things.

The Attempt

I gasp at the solitude of love.
Tears fall at the loss of a dream.
How can our world so pleasantly
Pretend that love is what it seems?

Is the sunset less beautiful
Because of the setting?
Is love less beautiful
If you fail in the getting?

Perhaps one day
I will climb and not fall.
Perhaps I'll find love
Like my dreams after all.

Hurting You

My hand is red…
stained
from the blood
you bled
when I cut you
with my sharp nails.
You were holding my hand.
I dug my nails
into your flesh
to make you loosen your grip.
I could not watch
My own painful actions.
But I had to help you
let me go.
Before we both fell
from the edge
of the cliff.

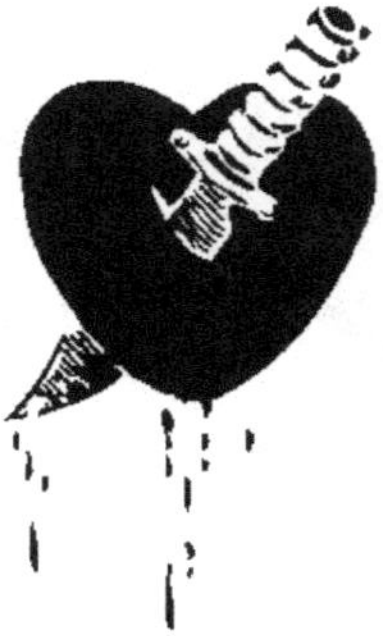

Patient

Blessing me in
Bleeding sorrow
Will you wait
For me tomorrow

Can't you see
That I am learning
While your broken
Heart I'm earning

Your Eyes

Your eyes tell me a story
That I invent at will.
Once I dreamed within them
That you would love me still.

Once while looking in them
I was shocked to find you there.
Truly, I had been quite lost—
Lost within your stare.

Now I have found the truth there
Where once were lies, at best.
My heart is finally learning
To lay her dreams to rest.

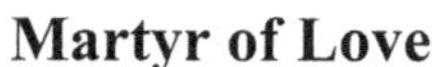

Martyr of Love

Martyr of Love
That is my name.
I must endure
The heartache and pain.

I can't give up.
I cannot say die.
My eyes to my heart
Continually lie.

Martyr of Love
No reason, no rhyme
Maybe the martyr
Will die yet this time.

A Fading Dream

I've dreamed of being dressed in white
And walking down the aisle.
I've dreamed of looking in his eyes
And seeing that proud smile.

Wedding bells and bridesmaids
A merry bridal shower,
Smiles, hugs and kisses
Until the final hour.

A marriage full of miracles,
Children, family, love.
This is what, each day and night,
I've been dreaming of.

But now this dream is fading;
As all dreams finally end.
I do not need a lover;
I only need a friend.

Heartbreaker

I played the game

of breaking hearts

until my heart

got broken.

Charmed

a chance meeting
a fleeting glance
a passing smile
I dream a dance

A simple handshake
a fragile line
you ignore another
my heart is thine

you pick my side
you look my way
a kindly comment
my heart does sway

then overlooked
you dance with another
the hug of a friend
not of a lover

what's on your mind?
could I lay claim?
O, such as you
as yet untamed

I must go on
ignore the harm
but can I learn
to ignore your charm?

My Heart

When I first saw you, my heart stood still.

When you finally saw me, my heart skipped a beat.

When I came to know you, my heart was touched.

When you whispered to me, my heart beat wildly.

But when you said goodbye, my heart was in my throat.

And when you left me, my heart broke.

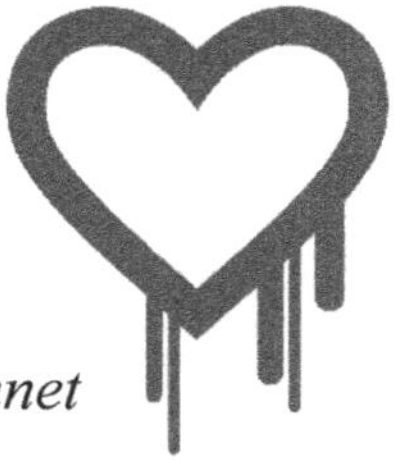

Let Me Forget

A Shakespearean Sonnet

A time will come when I will ask your name
And sigh for times I now can still recall.
A chance remembering of now the same
Will fade and skip along a mental wall.
Perchance I'll catch a glimpse of someone's face
That will in me a spark of memory give,
But likely this will not my heartbeat race;
Forgetting you is what I must to live.
And time will tell if loving is forgot.
There have been those who live the past alone.
A dreamer for what ended I am not.
I search the here and now to find my home.
But even as I look to future bliss…
As of today I long to feel your kiss.

Guilt

I can't find forgiveness;
I can't find rest.
There's a burning sorrow
inside my chest.

He does not love me.
It's in his eyes.
He thinks my heart
is full of lies.

How can I approach him?
What would I say?
Is it enough
to sit and pray?

Loneliness

I wake to find my arms empty,
my lips un-kissed
my soul unread
The very meaning of loneliness
Having believed you were loved
and having loved
but learning that, indeed,
you were never loved at all
and yet you still love
the shadow of what you knew
And I awake to find my arms empty,
my lips un-kissed,
my soul unread.

When I Love You

When I love you,
I love myself
Loving you.
When I see you,
I see and like myself
Through your eyes.
When I impress you,
I am impressed
By my own charm.
When I deceive you,
I am shocked
At my own skill.
But when I glance
My trap for you
Of impending pain,
I know this must end—
And soon…
But how I will miss
Your loving
Me.

Silence

This silence
is like no other.
It is empty—
          frightening—
          lonely.
I call out your name—
…but like a teardrop in the sea
my voice is lost
in vast emptiness
and quickly consumed
by this hungry silence.

This silence
is deafening—
          confining—
          joyless.
You could not hear me
--even if I screamed
with all my might.
I am

          alone…

alone and empty—
like the silence I am in.

Kneeling Roses

When I pass—
Ironic reverence—
Even the roses kneel.

Thorns bend up
Like the hands
Of a jester's bow.

They die to me
As if in spite.
Each simple pleasure steal.

But as they go—
Deny me love—
As if I could know how.

~ *Creativity* ~

The Poem Box

There is a poem box someplace,
Though I do not know where.
It's locked away by sacred key
Of which there is no spare.

It could be in the atmosphere
Or stolen by the sea.
Perhaps it's lost upon the land—
So precious—but it's free!

I know there is a leak in it,
For poems have been found.
Sometimes people, as they roam,
Will spot one on the ground.

Some will recognize them fast
And write them down to keep.
Others will ignore their shine
And away the poems seep.

It seems this poem box, though lost,
Has yet so much to show.
Each poem that escapes its cage
Will find in whom to grow.

These poems can roam long and far
Once they have gotten free.
They could find 'bout anyone;
In fact, a few found me.

Creating

In some far off place
My children play.
They cry.
They love.
Their ruler is
My imagination.
My every whim—
Their destiny.
I've the power
To grant life
Or shower death.
I've the right
To bless with joy
Or curse with sorrow.

But I like lovers…
Kisses…
Marriage.
I like for them to
Find true joy in God.

I like happy endings.

But plots must be realistic.
Not all can be
Fairy tales for me—
For I know that
Life is not a fairytale,
But a test… and even
Fairytales have villains.

And so my children
Will learn of pain
Sorrow,
Death.
Some will not survive—
And I shed tears for them.
For I feel their despair.
But others will conquer
With God's help
And my blessing.
They will love and laugh—
And I with them.
For they are me.

Lost Poems

A poem is
The gentle shine
In mass of muddled thoughts.
If it isn't
Trapped in words,
Then it is soon forgot.
How many poems
Have been lost,
For lack
Of pen and sheet?
How many wonders
And ideas
Will we never meet?

Dream Poetry

Our knowledge,
Feelings,
And our views
Combine to form
Our dreams.
This is poetry,
My friend.
This is what
It means.

I wonder if
I dream
In verse.
Do my
Thought waves
Rhyme?
If I stole
My poems thus,
Would it be
A crime?

Writing

I have breathed the breath of life
By use of sheet and pen.
Two worlds connect upon the page
And here new times begin.

Have I not created thus
Another world in truth?
Have they not come to exist
Throughout my dreams since youth?

And so they live their written lives
In dimensions you can't see—
Unless you find them in a book—
Unless you start to read.

~ Identity ~

Different Shadows

Each light makes a different shadow,
Each life a different past.
Every seed has different offspring,
Every ship a different mast.

Each rock has a different shape,
Each song a different tune.
Every bride wears a different smile,
Every world, a different moon.

A light cannot bear offspring.
A seed cannot give light.
A stone cannot go sailing
Across the sea at night.

So show me all your colors,
Between the black and white.
Let all your strengths shine through
And bloom out into sight.

And do not fight the limits
That God lets on you rest.
Be content and full of joy
That you will pass the test.

Both of Me

Susan is more sensible.
She's caring and she's kind.
But Sue is wild, so carefree,
And tends to lose her mind.

Susan never takes the lead,
But Sue is first to speak.
Susan waits and makes a guess,
But sometimes Sue will peak.

Susan gets quite nervous
And is so often shy.
Sue lives for adventure.
Her courage will not die.

Susan writes the poetry;
Sue will act it out.
Susan is the quiet one;
Sue will laugh and shout.

Susan is more motherly;
Sue more like the child.
Susan is the thoughtful one;
Sue is purely wild.

Susan knows something of life
And longs for wisdom most.
Sue will play and live by chance.
Her charms she'll freely boast.

Susan smiles and sings a song.
Sue gets up to dance.
Susan waits quite patiently,
But Sue longs for romance.

The girls are truly different;
Susan, normal; Sue, so odd!
But in heart they're quite the same.
They've learned to trust in God.

Expression

Each breath, a survival note

Each tear, an expression

Each sigh, trying to accept

Each look, a confession

Each word I write, a symbol

Each song I sing, a view

Each word I speak, a struggle

But no one sees the truth.

~ Love & Marriage ~

And this is love...

And this is love...
how you look at me
and tell me how you feel,
how you are always
aware of my needs
and desires,
And how, now,
as I see you,
tired and weary,
helping me
by cleaning my kitchen,
hunched over
assembling that crib,
moving it carefully
to another room
so I can sleep.
And I see the care you take
and the joy you find,
knowing you are of help to me
and the little one—
the baby girl—
who isn't even yours
...and this is love.

Midnight Serenade

The world around me
starts to fade
at your midnight
serenade.

Love was but
a mere charade
'til your midnight
serenade.

Songs of love
You slowly played
Through your midnight
serenade.

Then to you
I gently bade.
Love my midnight
serenade.

Blush

A twinkle glistens in your eye.
You breathe a small and gentle sigh.
A smile plays along your brow.
My heart beats out a secret vow.

Your laughter dances on the breeze.
Your eyes wink a happy tease.
Your glance sets my heart on fire.
A blush uncovers my desire.

Choose

If you decide to leave me now,
I'll open up the door.
If you decide to take your bow,
I will not beg for more.

So, if you choose to run away,
I will set you free.
But, if you choose not to stay,
Do not look back to me.

Doubts

A glimpse at my heart
A sign from my soul
I've shown him my pleasure,
My heartache, my goal.

The truth behind my laughter
The reasons for my pain
What he's seen in me
I hope was not in vain.

My questions go unanswered.
Doubts loom up inside.
Should I run and dance for joy
Or should I run and hide?

Your Picture

To see your face; my only choice,
Yet how I long to hear your voice.

I look at you; you cannot see
My loneliness and misery.

Your body—still, yet so alive!
A twinkle captured in your eyes.

Your arms are strong, yet far away.
I won't be held in them today.

It is a window, not a door.
Your picture makes me miss you more.

Dream Ghost

Your voice is like an echo in the night.
Startled from my rest I run to find you.
I search the woods; and find you're not in sight.
Perhaps you've found someone else to run to.
I feel a motion close against my side.
Have you always been here right beside me?
Who could it be that I heard in the night?
Could it be the dream ghost come to haunt me?
If I yet I know I have you in my life,
Why do my dreams keep me searching for you?
And still this question cuts me like a knife—
To wonder if I'm the one you'd run to.

I Lost My Love

I'll seek to see
if I might find
the love I lost
deep in your eyes.

Perhaps I'll find
the love I miss
when searching for it
in your kiss.

Risk

How I despise
This cage
I've locked my heart into.
How I loathe
My inability to be loved—
To love unchecked.
Safety—is it worth the loneliness?
Love—is it worth the risk?

Seeking

A yearning deep inside of me
A longing in my soul
A burning at the heart of me
Your touch would make me whole

The passion of my gentle youth
The caution of years past
Now I am seeking for the truth
I need this love to last

Your glance will set my heart ablaze
A spark to light the fire
Surely my eyes the truth display
Do you see my desire?

When…

When the rain turns to glass
    As if falls through the sky
When the bird learns to speak
    And the whale learns to fly,
When the rock starts to bleed,
    And the flower to cry—
That's when my love for you
    Will die.

When the wolverine wants
    To be your best friend,
When the mocking bird falls
    In love with a wren,
When the dog learns to purr
    And the tree learns to bend,
That's when my love for you
    Will end.

When the sheep turns around
    And sheers its own fleece,
When the mountain goat flies
    Down south with the geese,
When the sunshine brings darkness
    And the famished shark peace,
That's when my love for you
    Will cease.

Missing You

A sigh escapes
My tightened chest
My heart beats true
Within my breast.

Your face, though still
I see each day.
There is so much
I'd like to say.

Though out of grasp
I think of you.
You rule my dreams
The whole night through.

There is a place
I long to be:
Safe in your arms,
Held guardingly.

My Love for You

My love for you
does not rest

in your kisses
in your touch
in your eyes
or even in your heart.

My love for you
does not rest

in your reactions to me
in your feelings
in you.

My love for you
belongs to me.
It remains alive
with or without
you returning it,

and it does not
rest.

Words

I'm sitting here
In my class—
English Grammar
—so needed
—so complicated
—so essential to all communication

Who cares?

The communication
I have with you
Doesn't always need words
Or English grammar
Or rules
That are always broken anyway.

Is love a word?
Must it be
Conjugated
Manipulated
Elaborated
To be
Expressed?
Can't you just look at me
And know?

Such As I

At night alone,
Awake I lie.
Why should you care
For such as I?

I am so young.
So much to learn.
A chance at love.
Is it my turn?

You are so sure.
I am so shy.
Why should you care
For such as I?

Is this a dream,
Or is it true?
Could I be truly
Loved by you?

At night alone,
Awake I lie.
Why should you care
For such as I?

Strength in Two

Why do you cry
O lover of mine?
I see your tears,
So restless inside.

Sometimes I wish
That you were so near
I could relieve
Each sorrow, each fear.

Every breath you take
Would be as if mine.
Each shift of my soul
Would be as if thine.

If I could but hear
Each whisper, each dream
No secrets between us;
How perfect it seems.

But then I must stop
To look once again.
You can't lose yourself
In me, my true friend.

We both must learn
To stand on our own.
I'll still be near;
You won't be alone.

I'll fail at times.
I'm not quite that strong.
And then sometimes
You'll help me along.

Together we'll grow.
There's more strength in two.
You'll thank God for me.
I'll thank God for you.

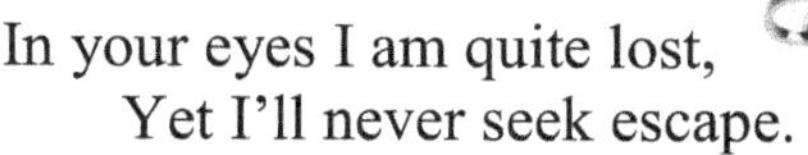

In Your Eyes

In your eyes I am quite lost,
    Yet I'll never seek escape.

In your eyes I am disarmed,
    Yet I'll never wish to fight.

In your eyes, I am falling,
    Though I never want to land.

In your eyes, I am drawn in,
    But I'll never pull away.

In your eyes I am drowning,
    But I'll never claim a breath.

In your eyes I am a captive,
    But I'll never loose my chains.

Though I may not find true love,
In your eyes my heart remains.

Too Gloomy

There once was a man who was unhappy and gloomy.
And his wife complained that the house was too roomy,
Or that he never invited his boss home for dinner,
Or when he played golf he was never the winner…
Or that the back yard was a little too small,
Or that the pet dog was a little too tall…
Or maybe they needed a new kitchen stool,
Or maybe he needed to put in a pool—
But whatever the problem or what the complaint,
The biggest one was—he wasn't a saint!
And so he was gloomy day in and day out,
And the gloomier he was, the more she would shout,
"Why don't you get up and start moving about?!
You don't love me at all!" And then she would pout.
So finally he couldn't take any more.
So he packed up his bags, and he walked out the door.
And he packed up his wallet and packed up his car,
And he drove to the beach—away—very far.
And there he stayed for all of that day.
He laid on the beach, and he took in the rays.
He played in the sand, and he swam in the sea.
He sailed in the wind, and he drank his sun-tea.
And then as the sun was sinking to land,
He looked for someone to tell, "Life is grand!"
…But no one was there. He was very alone.
And suddenly, then, he longed to go home.
And as he was driving back home from the sea
He realized something… "Life isn't just ME."
And so he decided that the very next day
He would rescue his wife from another sad day,
And together they'd come to this beautiful beach—
Which isn't quite so nice without someone in reach,

And they would forget that the house was too roomy,
And they would forget to be unhappy and gloomy.
Because the beach was great! —And it wasn't raining!
And life is too short to spend time complaining!

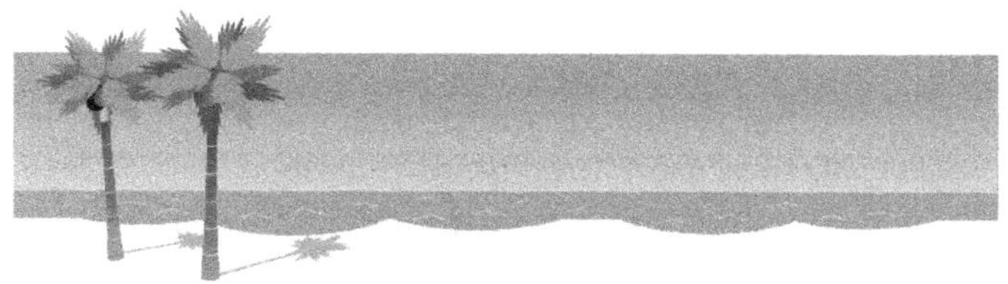

The Journey

I've gazed into a pond and seen
    My own face staring back at me.
I've traveled 'round a lonely bend
    And still I did not find a friend.
I've slept beneath the open sky
    And added to it my own sigh.
And then, just as my searching ceased,
    I found a God that still loved me.

He knew my heart and all my needs.
    He saw all that I did not see.
He took my cares and dried my tears.
    He gave me strength to persevere.
He taught my soul to love Him most
    And how to only in Him boast.
And just as I loved Him anew,
    He turned around and gave me you.

The Lesson

When you asked me to marry
I could not contain my tears.
Such joy was nearly painful.
The dream of coming years.
The day holds so much meaning:
Our respect, joy and love.
Since then, our future marriage
Is what I'm dreaming of.
But God started a lesson
That first sweet day we met;
Leading us to share this day
To become one—and yet,
Our lesson isn't over;
We're learning to be one.
Then one day, when comes the King,
We'll be joined with His Son.
So now in preparation
For the great coming King,
God chose to build this marriage.
To you I'll always cling.
As I look into your eyes
I see His love for me.
I get to learn this lesson
With none other, friend, than thee.

~ Humor & Whimsy ~

How I Met Your Mom

This is based on a story my Navajo father-in-law often tells about how he met my white mother-in-law. (She just rolls her eyes.)

My brothers and I,
Young Indian braves,
Were out on the prairie
One midsummer day.
We looked to the east
And off far away
We saw a wagon train
Heading our way.
Swarthy and lonely,
Our heads started swimmin'.
We said to each other,
"Let's go get the women!"
So, we jumped on our horses
We all raced away,
But it seems my luck
Was not with me that day.
My horse was the slowest.
He ran like he slept.
And when I arrived
She was all that was left.

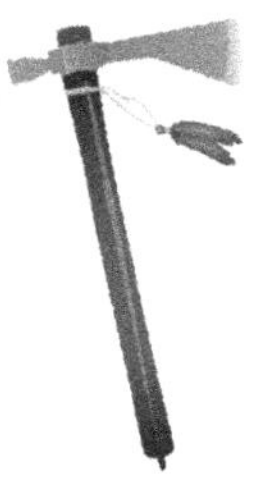

Peanut Butter

Spread the peanut butter well.
Love that peanut butter smell!
Crunchy makes me munch my bread,
But the smooth is fun to spread,
Back and forth across the bread,
Making visions in my head,
Of the taste I dream of most.
It goes well with fruit or toast.
And with chocolate it's fine.
Makes me dream, *It's mine, all mine!*
Now it's getting nice and thick.
Maybe I could take a lick…
Just one taste before I'm done,
Licking fingers, one by one.
Now the jar is all I see.
Too bad this one's not for me.

Joe-Stud

My name is Joe-Stud
And I'm here to say,
I've got a great bod
And I like it that way.

I've got a big pool
With a nice, sunny deck
And the girls can't wait
Until I flex my pecks!

I lay in the sun
To work on my tan.
And the girls won't look
At any other man.

I've got a big broad chest
And a lot of muscle.
Whenever I call
All the girls sure hustle!

There are redheads, blonds
And many brunettes.
There isn't a girl
That I couldn't get.

I don't have a big ego—
Just a good self-esteem.
But when the girls see me
They practically scream!

The Train

Chug-a, chug-a, chug-a, chug!
We've been waiting! Here it comes!
Red lights flashing; arm drops down
So to safely pass through town.
It's in sight now, moving fast!
Churning wind! Blazing past!
I can hear it, horn so loud!
Like a roaring orca crowd!
Ground is shaking! Cars whizz by!
I might count them, if I try.
Sis was sleeping, now awake.
Eyes are wide, mouth agape!
Cars go stretching round the bend.
They keep coming! There's no end!
My heart goes thumping—thud, thud, thud!
With that chug-a, chug-a, chug!

Fairy Song

On the open prairie
A rushing wind did call.
Flit a mountain fairy
Through misty waterfall.

Spellbound ladies singing;
The lilies bade them near.
Through the valleys ringing;
A song of grace to hear.

The Whistler

He roamed the world
to whistled tune.

He whistled morning,
evening, noon.

He whistled under
stars and moon.

He danced his dance
to whistled tune.

~ *Faith & Spirituality* ~

Hoax or History?

Was Jesus man or mythology?
Clever hoax or Divine Majesty?
And if He isn't all He claimed
how have such lies so long remained?

How did they find such a perfect one
to masquerade as God's own Son?
And who could fulfill all prophesies
of line and birth and family?

How did He ever find escape
from those who might claim a mistake?
Not friends or neighbors—little brothers—
rivals, enemies or any others?

How did they ever fake the way
He healed the sick against the fray
of religious leaders who would love to see
Him forced to return to Galilee?

And did He really raise the dead
or heal the sick without *one* shred
of evidence to support the fact
that He was nothing but a hack?

And how could enemies of state
fake His return from beyond the grave?
And then manufacture lies
that He appeared before their eyes?

And also appeared to 500 others?
How did they control such astounding numbers?
And to claim all this in a tiny place,
yet no one dared deny their case?

How did they spread the written lies
before His witnesses' very eyes?
And yet there wasn't even one
who claimed the accounts were somehow wrong?

Now, even though these men were false
we cannot prove the truth at all?
For where is the proof Jesus never existed?
Or at least some evidence His claim was invented?

I want to know, so tell me, please,
How does one fake archeology?
And how have the Scriptures stood so long
when so many are certain they are wrong?

Despite our vast technology
and knowledge of our history,
I sincerely doubt anyone today
could make such a claim and get away.

Others have tried, and so we know,
that a clever writer or mind-control
is sooner or later brought to light
and others are warned of its blight.

And yet this Jesus blows the mind!
How could a whole nation become blind?
And then a region? And then the world—
come to call this man the Lord?

I think I'll take another look
into this very strange, old Book,
and see if I might find the fault
that those before me never caught.

For I have a very clever mind!
What others lose, I often find!
...But, yet, I must admit to you...
At times I worry it might be true....

Deliverance

I once was offered
A chance to be free.
A choice to make—
Who did I want to be?

I looked to my friends.
They wanted to play.
But when I was hurt
They all turned away.

I chose an old path,
So smooth and so wide.
Yet, would it fulfill
The hollow inside?

I laughed and I danced.
I had my own way.
I made love to sin
'till that fateful day.

The road I was on
Came to a dead end.
I had no true joy,
No purpose, no friend.

And then I looked up.
I saw a new road.
It was narrow and steep,
But so lighter the load!

And then a scarred hand
Reached down from above.
I learned of such mercy,
Such peace and such love.

Once I had dreamed
And longed to be free.
But my soul was trapped
In evil liberty.

I was so lost
And I could not see
'Till God helped me live
When He died for me.

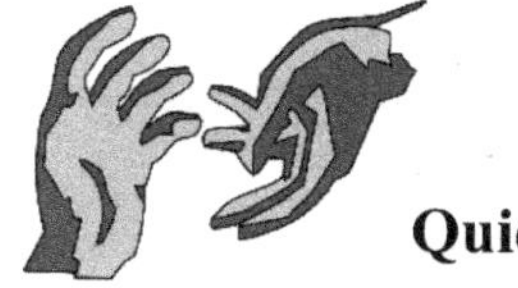

Quiet Time

A silent place,
no one around.
I hear Your voice,
but not a sound.

May your Spirit
guide my eyes.
May I never
trust in lies.

You can hear me
when I pray.
Teach me how
to trust each day.

The Mist

A mist has settled on this life I lead
shadowing over the tears I bleed.

My eyes are strained as I search to find
I know not what is in this mist that blinds.

The future hovers at hand, and yet,
I was not ready for this mist to set.

All words are muffled though kindly said.
They float like ghosts inside my head.

And yet my reason, though now obscure,
whispers something—I am not sure.

Perhaps it was inborn in me,
or taught when I was young and free.

Or, maybe, it is something new.
That I had known but never knew.

That even when the mist grows dense
and thought and words have lost their sense

that mists—no matter how thick they grow—
can never last forever... no.

It must subside and allow the Light
to pierce its struggle to keep the night.

And when the sun comes out at last,
I may look back to this dark past

and see what I had missed before
when I had searched for something more.

For in the searching I must have lost
the simple joys the mist has cost.

And now I seem to realize
with gently healing tearful eyes

that before this mist I walked not free;
a greater mist overshadowed me.

For this was one I did not know
that slowly pushed my joy down low.

And only now with this great cloud
can I perceive through foggy shroud

that when joy comes it's not regained,
for I have never yet attained

the fullest peace and warmest grace
that best shines in the darkest place.

And though this mist has yet to rise
and though the tears still cloud my eyes,

I can rely on Jesus Name—
who for me died and for me came.

For He went through a darkness still
worse than I have or ever will.

So in this setting mist and pain
which I endure each morn again.

I'll pray as I watch this mist slowly rise
that I'll see anew with His own eyes.

Hold My Hand, Lord

Hold my hand
So I won't fall.
Hold my hand
And I'll stand tall.

Hold my hand
So I won't fear.
Hold my hand.
I'll know You're near.

Hold my hand
So I can trust.
Hold my hand.
Oh, please, You must!

Hold my hand.
I love You so.
Hold my hand.
Help my love grow.

Forgiveness

God says I am forgiven
as far as east to west,
but consequences of my sin
will give my soul no rest.

My problems seem no smaller,
my doubts are growing still.
Can't I ever find true peace?
It seems I never will.

Some said it would be easy;
my faults would disappear.
Then, why do I still battle?
Why should my heart still fear?

But God is living in me
leaving sins upon the shelf.
I know that He forgave me.
I must forgive myself.

Guardian for the Son

The assembly came before the Lord,
And silence filled the place.
There was no shuffling of wings,
No smile on a face.

Each creature stood in trembling,
Hoping only for the best.
They had worked so very hard
So they might pass the test.

And now the time had come at last
For God to choose the one.
The angel from the crowd that would
Be guardian to His Son.

One by one they filed past
And God asked them as they came,
"Why do you want to become
the Guardian to my Name?"

The angels spoke of worship grand,
Of protection and of joy.
They spoke about their qualities
And dreams to guard the Boy.

The Lord God seemed quite pleased,
But the questioning went on
Until at last upon the stage
There stepped a tiny one.

The Lord's voice boomed and questioned
Him in front of everyone,

"Why do you think you are he
Who should protect my Son?"

The tiny angel bowed quite low.
At first he did not speak.
Then at last he raised his eyes,
The Father's face to seek.

"Because I love You with all the love
That You have given me.
And if I could lay down my life,
I'd do it willingly.

"If only I could have the chance
To in some small measure show
That all I'll ever want for me
Is that my love for You will grow."

The Lord was silent, the room stood still
And Heaven held its breath.
It was like those times on Earth,
When a sinner meets with death.

Then at last God smiled;
And His smile was pure light.
He said, "I've found the one of you
That will see my Son tonight."

Then God formed a special star
That would shine for all to see,
And a chorus of angels began to sing
A joyous jubilee.

The cry was heard of God's dear Child,
Born down on Earth for men.
The tiny angel quickly came
To the stable of an inn.

He was the first of angels
To look upon God's face.
And then, unseen at Jesus' side,
He knelt and worshipped Grace.

Through the Glass

A Shakespearean Sonnet

He must become greater; I must become less.
John 3:30

Its shimmer and its promise draw me near.
A spark within prompts me toward what I see.
I find the eyes of one I love and fear;
She's gazing out of my eyes back at me.
How long I stood there I cannot recall
To contemplate what beauty I might find
And search out every blemish, every flaw
To bind them each securely in my mind.
But had I chanced to look beyond my face
I would have gazed into another's eyes,
For there He stood with patience and with grace
To teach me how to see through all the lies.
Forever He will beckon and will bade.
To see Him I must search and I must fade.

His Gift To You

Each day when I think about you
I ask God that you'll see
How much He truly loves you.
I ask on bended knee.

The King was scoffed at, flogged and whipped.
His flesh was torn apart.
Yet the agony he bravely took,
Since He loved you from the start.

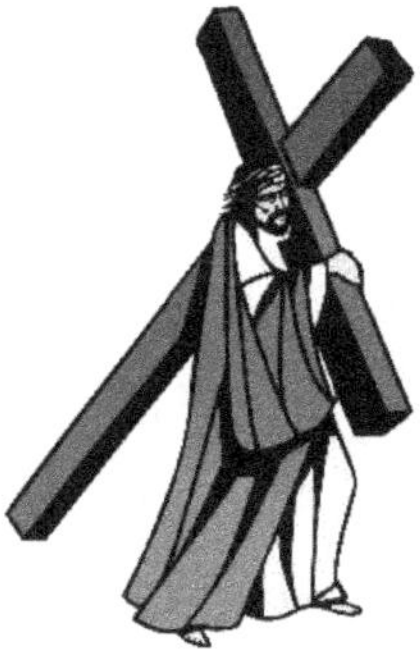

He was raised high upon a cross
Made of the strongest wood.
Yet nothing had He done in life
Except the pure and good.

He loves you oh so deeply.
You could never understand.
He watched the blood run down
His arms and soak into the sand.

His robe was stolen and lots
Were cast by the wicked men.
But He raised His eyes and asked
For their forgiveness even then.

He finally died with a crown of thorns
Pressed down upon His head.
But three days later, from the grave,
He rose up from the dead.

He did not have to die that day,
Yet He chose to set you free
From all your guilt and sin and shame
To give you liberty.

Wandering

I wandered o'er a mountain,
I wandered 'cross the sea,
I wandered through a valley
Where I met you wandering.

Then together we went wandering,
As wanderers will do,
But soon I realized, with fright,
I'd wandered 'way from you.

So then I started searching
And exploring as I went.
God taught me then a lesson
That I'll not soon forget.

I searched the whole word over
And found you finally.
You had stopped your wandering
And had begun to search for me.

So wandering is wonderful
If wandering's all you do;
But you don't need to wander,
If God is leading you.

Security

Corrosion cannot
Touch my soul.
For God, my Lord,
Will make me whole.

He has his hand
Around my life.
To Him my joy,
My grief, my strife.

Hope

At the point of discovery I may find loss.
I pray I learn to look to the cross.

At the point of triumph shall I now fail?
It seems that all is to no avail.

I've gained such wisdom yet I feel a fool.
Will I never learn love can be cruel?

If I must, I'll learn to cope.
But I'll never learn to give up hope.

Will You, God?

Will You give me wisdom
when I need it most?
Will You give me humility?
I should not boast.

Will You give me strength
to do what's right?
Will You guide me through
the dark of night?

Will You hold my hand
as I walk along?
Will You fill my heart
with joyful song?

Will You give me courage
to face my fears?
Will you wipe away
my shameful tears?

I know You love me.
I know You care.
And I will find
my answers there.

Faith

Corrosion cannot
touch my soul.
For God, my Lord,
will make me whole.

He has His hand
upon my life.
To him my joy,
my grief, my strife.

Love Thoughts

I always know when I'm in your thoughts.
No matter where I am,
the sun shines brighter,
the birds sing sweeter
and roses fill the land.
If, perhaps, the wind smells sweet,
or rain cools the day,
I realize with a sigh and smile,
your thoughts have bent my way.
Any simple blessing nature can perform,
I know what lies behind it—
the love thoughts of the Lord.

Pride

Pride, who are you?
I believe you are at the
core of every sin,
every want,
every need.
How can I find true humility—
while directly striving
to be humble?
My nature is thus,
yet I harbor no excuses.
Though I inherited my sinfulness
I am no less trapped by it
than were those who left it
to me.
And thus, I see my need.
And thus, I search for an escape.
And thus, I find His freedom
from you.

~ Honoring Loved Ones ~

Breathe Easy

A Shakespearean Sonnet
For My Grandpa, O. Carl Brown,
who died after a long battle
with pulmonary fibrosis.
November 26, 1918 – November 12, 2010

For hope based in the promise of his King,
For love lacking not height nor width nor depth,
By faith in grace that covers everything,
He shamelessly blessed Christ's Name with each breath.
When times of joy and peace and laughter came
And when that happy laughter turned to loss—
When sorrow came to visit or to stay—
He breathed in that fragrant, bittersweet cross.
Not wanting to keep secret his great joy
Or fearing trials or what man might say,
He shared Christ with man, woman, girl and boy
And lived in times that took his breath away.
Now at home in pastures fresh and breezy
With his Christ, he finally breathes easy.

I Hope To Be…

There is one who encourages
When I feel insecure.
She knows that to understand
And listen is the cure.

I am one to be sought out
With perseverance and a goal.
This one chose to love with strength,
Though hidden was my soul.

This one is so proud of me
Though I might lose my way.
She will calmly point to God.
"Trust Him," she'll simply say.

This one stresses discipline
With love and mercy sweet.
The medicine will not taste bad
If given with a treat.

She teaches and exhorts me.
She provides for every need.
Generously she gives herself,
Planting love just like a seed.

I love you for your patience
And the love you've given me.
Now I pray I'll learn someday,
To such a mother be.

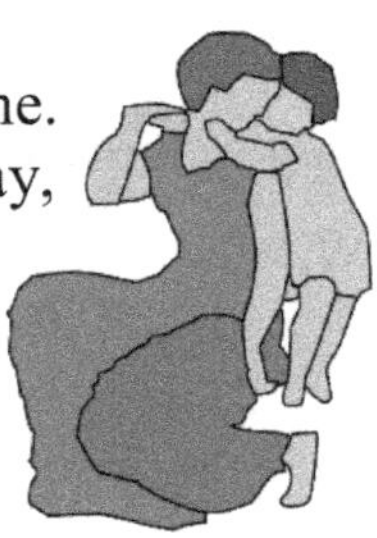

~ Death & Legacy ~

Child in a Cemetery

A rusty
Fence the only
wall. So underneath
I had to crawl. But then a
new wall met my heart. It beat
so fast. Such fear, what art? A
memory is pushed aside. Its shadow,
though, caused me to hide. I saw the
stone—so old and calm. I crept up slow.
whispered a psalm. Grotesque stories rushed
my brain; of lack of love, of bodies slain.
Now upon their graves I stand. But forever
shall they roam this land… until their memory
is forgot. I shan't be he, for ne'er it ought.

Death Wish

Dancing now and free from pain

Everlasting joy to claim

All my tears are wiped away

Total love I've found this day

How I've longed, this place to see

Death, a wish to worship Thee.

Ode To The Fort Collins Dam

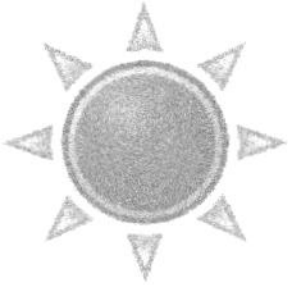

She sat in the hot shade

Of her Hogan on that day

In the smell of dust and dung

And smoothly talked her native tongue

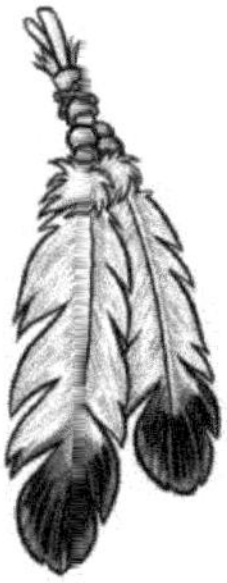

Of the grass, tall and green,

Of the water in the stream

Of the beauty of the place,

A sad smile on her face…

'Cause as I looked around

I saw nothing but the ground,

And patches of sage and brush

And broken trucks and such.

For when they built the dam—

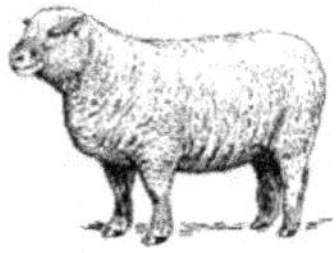

Not quite on Navajo land—

They cared not what was lost

Or of those who'd pay the cost.

Death

When he comes a'knocking
I will not hesitate.
I'll open up the door to him
And gladly face my fate.

He won't be ugly or dressed in black.
White roses he will show.
And when he gently speaks my name,
I will surely go.

And then we'll reach that glorious place.
The journey won't be long.
He'll hold my hand, and in we'll come,
To hear the angel song.

Indian Tomb

I chanced to pass an Indian tomb—
A mound so large, there must be room
For sixteen trucks to therein hide
With room for wagons there, beside.
To top this mound a gazebo stood
With little help to tend the mood
Of Indian rites and old death chants,
Of sacred song and Indian dance.

I wondered as I passed thereby
What sort of things might therein lie.
Were beaded chains and settled moans
Still wound around those Indian bones?
Did women hold their babies nigh
When at the birth they both had died?
And were the ancients laid up close
To all the ones they loved the most?

Had Indian chiefs laid up a store
Of all their gold and wealth galore?
Or would one dig down deep to see
A piece of broken pottery?
Had artists of that time of old
Conserved the art from broken molds?
And did the men of medicine
Here hide the cures for what ails men?

How many wonders might be found
Beneath that secret Indian mound?
But did the tribe set up a curse
And chant it to the mound in verse
To keep away the greedy men

Who might disturb their Indian kin?
And all these thoughts did through me fly.
I looked again, and passed on by.

~ *Miscellaneous Poems* ~

Now

Now.
I feel it slipping
away; it never stops;
always slipping; yet it
never actually leaves;
always changing
present,
being,
doing,
changing;
oily water
slipping through
the tightest grasp;
always slipping
never gone.
Now.

Crowd

I'm caught in a crowd of people,
but no one knows my name.
Everyone is different,
but everyone's the same.

In Heaven Too Soon

When I got to Heaven, I asked God
Why I was there so soon.

I had never seen a sunset,
A morning star or the moon.

I had never tasted something sweet
Or smelled a budding rose.

I had never held a purring cat
Or felt sand run through my toes.

He answered me quite gently,
And tears glistened as He said,

“Your parents didn’t understand
that for you My blood was shed.

“You’ll be happy here forever,
Though you never lived your life.

“You’ll never have to cry a tear
or suffer or have strife

“But never will you understand
the joy to work for Me.

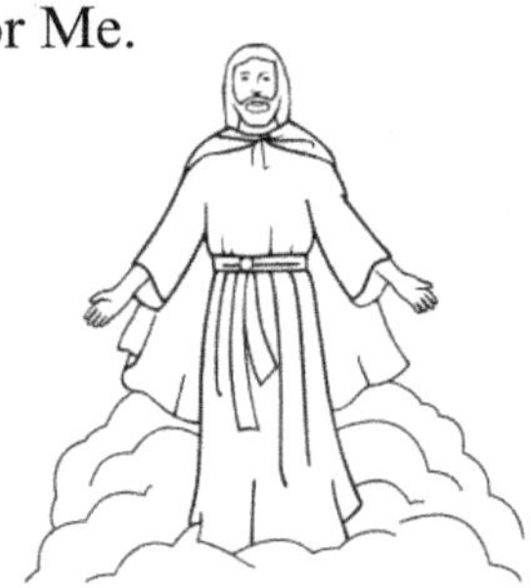

"The struggles you will never bear,
but some blessings you'll never see."

I wished somehow I could return
And explain to my parents why

It was so wrong to kill a child;
One too young to die.

Of course, I have forgiven them
But My Father will not forget,

Until my parents believe in Christ,
Who has already paid their debt.

Though I was killed quite painfully
Before I could be born,

I can understand my parents' pain
And for them, I truly mourn.

They do not have to be depressed,
Feel forgotten or alone.

They can find forgiveness, peace, rest
And the joy that Christ has shown.

The Clock

You see him,
His arms reaching out
In a desperate effort
To bridge the gap
To touch the edge
Of his world, his face
He turns here and there
He stretches across time
And space
But never will he succeed
It is not in his destiny
It is not in his making
Behind glass he stares—
So fragile, fragile yet confining—
And gives of himself
His livelihood
But never will he be complete
Never will he touch the edge
Never will time end
For him.

Ode to Tijuana
and Her Sister Cities World Over

Side by side
Row upon row
Colorful refuse homes
A mountainside decorated with poverty
Survival—the only luxury
Sweat stained rags cover dusty bodies
Shoeless children
Evil ribcage dogs
Buzzards circle overhead
In the white heat
Above the sound and smell of defeat
The city dump
Playground
Workplace
Gathering
The trucks don't stop
Not even for the child in the way
Lost in the maze of litter
Searching for gems, unaware
They wash my windshield
Braid my hair
Sell me churros,
Chiclets
Fish tacos
Handmade jewelry, pottery
A cross with a tiny slain Jesus
Their lives
One trinket at a time
So I can remember
My fun-filled vacation

Giving

I once walked down a lonely way,
passed a beggar as I went.
Her palms stretched out as if to pray.
Some coins I gladly spent.

I kept on walking and I met
a young man with a frown.
His robes were finely tailored, yet
his features were cast down.

I gave a smile—it was returned.
I went my merry way.
I wish I'd seen the heart that yearned
For me to stop that day.

I passed an older woman frail,
who cried and coughed a bit.
I handed her my napkin, stale;
found her a chair to sit.

I walked along, whistled a tune,
but tired as I went.
The night came in without the moon.
The road secretly bent.

I stumbled cross a rocky way.
I fell upon the road.
All night in helpless pain I lay
'till last the sun did show.

I waited there for quite some time
for one to pass my way.
Surely someone would help me find
a place where I could stay.

Then finally I saw someone.
He quickly drew quite near.
I was so glad he'd finally come!
He knelt beside my ear.

He smiled, "Do get better friend.
I hope you find your way."
But just as quickly as he'd come,
He left me where I lay.

World of Glass

A silent cloud is sleeping
upon a world of glass.
A quiet bomb is creeping
among the blades of grass.
A watchful killer in the midst
of people who are blind.
A question mark begins the list
of things to take to mind.
So if you do not understand,
or if you do not care,
you might travel from this land
and meet your maker there.

Dangerous Charm

A fog sets in that rakes my soul.
The foam-tipped waves do roll and roll.
I look across this flattened rage.
A wild creature fights her cage.
An evil hand now rocks the boat,
And then it presses about my throat.
The winds rise up and tear the sails.
The waters boil, as in old tales.
The angry sea now fights us down,
And tries to force all life to drown.
Then finally she loses hate,
And in her arms she cradles fate.
She shows her beauty charm once more,
Thus, keeps our hearts away from shore.

Misogyny

A Shakespearean Sonnet

You smile at me and look me up and down
Forgetting that I'm as human as you.
I can't be seen nor can I make a sound
Lest I usurp the power you are due.
You preach at me that I must always yield.
For women are weak, mind, body and soul.
And claim that only will I be fulfilled
If you hold all the power and control.
You proof-text your position with great skill
Claiming God has always been on your side.
For no one can love women with strong wills.
Even God has his favorites, you lie.
But you seem to forget Christ set me free
When you call oppression equality.

About the Author

S. E. Thomas, M.A.

is a multi-published, award-winning, author, editor, and publisher. A wife, mother, and avid story-teller, she lives and works in Lolo, Montana. She has her master's degree in philosophy, is working on a seminary degree, and writes biblical historical fiction, inspirational fiction, YA dystopia, Christian drama, Christian non-fiction, poetry, and more. Susan is married to Dr. Aaron Thomas, and they have three children: Yesenia, Dakota, and Novik.

Please follow her author's page on Amazon and connect with her via Facebook and Twitter at:

www.facebook.com/AuthorSEThomas
@susanethomas1

More From:

@TDPPress
www.thedramaticpen.com
facebook.com/thedramaticpen

**Into the Beautiful
Poetry by Montana
Artists Series**

"Into the Beautiful: Poetry by Montana Artists" is a series of poetry books by Montana artists of all ages. These works of art and creativity were collected through annual contests run August through October 15th. To find out more about this contest, please visit our website at www.TheDramaticPen.com.

**Longing for Rest
A Novella
S. E. Thomas**

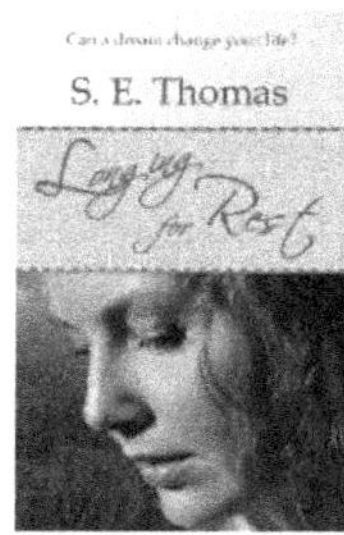

One heartbroken woman battles insomnia. Another cannot escape the coma trapping her between dreams and reality. Through a miraculous crossing of consciousness, they meet on a grassy hill surrounded by a mysterious fog. Here they form an unusual friendship. But will fear, pain, and betrayal spoil this haven? Will they finally be able to rest? Can a dream change your life? Available in paperback ($7.99) or eBook ($2.99 from Kindle or Nook.)

The Scrolls of the Nevi'im Series:

Book I: Habakkuk's Plea: A Prophet of Elohim
Book II: Habakkuk's Plea: Evil Persists
Book III: Habakkuk's Plea: Elohim Answers
S. E. Thomas

The Holy Land Mysteries Series

S. E. Thomas

Can Darash, a Jewish teenager, track a killer, rescue his family from ruin, and discover the truth about Yeshua? The rebel, Yeshua, drove the merchants from the Temple with a whip. Hours later, one of them was murdered. Now fifteen-year-old Darash must find a way to protect his family from poverty even as he struggles with the grief of losing his father. When another murder is committed, Darash finds himself searching for a dangerous killer and relying on an old, blind basket-weaver for help. Despite the odds, Darash discovers he has strength of character, a deep compassion for others, and an uncanny knack for problem-solving. But will he be able to expose the killer before the killer finds him?

Darash's adventures continue with…
Book I: The Sixth Hour
Book II: The Brazen Altar

Force Down the Night

Age of Technics Trilogy
S. E. Thomas

"I don't know why Absalom keeps me. I'm not any good at gene charting or chromosomal manipulation. My hands shake whenever I'm in the Fetal Growth Room. I can't even walk past the CC Surgery Center without feeling panicky and nauseous. There are too many buttons in this place—too many ways to end a life. And it scares me." Galaxy, a skinny fifteen-year-old girl with long white hair, doesn't know why Absalom spoils her so much. Especially since she's just an undersized CC—a member of the Commodity Class—a class of expendable slaves. When Galaxy discovers that Absalom is dying, she realizes her days of privilege are at an end. A new executive order will cut the CC population down by a third. Galaxy and her best friend, Needle, will be among those sent to the incineration chamber. Now Galaxy has a choice to make. Use what's left of her privilege to secure safety for herself and Needle… or join the doomed CC rebellion.

Who Invited The Stiff to Dinner?
An Interactive Mystery Party Game
for Teens and Adults
S. E. Thomas

The guests arrive for a distinguished dinner party at the wealthy English estate of Richard Orwell Mortice. But why would he invite so many of his enemies into his home, along with a Scotland Yard Inspector? When the maid discovers good ol' Rick O. Mortice dead, the Inspector and his overly eager Lieutenant sidekick are out to discover the culprit! Everyone has a motive, and the accusations fly—but not before they go ahead and sit down to a luxurious meal. After all, why let one stiff ruin dinner? *(Requires 15 participants.)*

Murder at Surly Gates
An Interactive Mystery Party Game
for Teens and Adults
S. E. Thomas

Tensions are high when the cantankerous residents of Surly Gates Nursing Home have to put up with money-hungry relatives, a spoiled brat, and her incompetent mother during visitors' hours. When the nursing home manager turns up dead in his office, everyone is a suspect! Who had something to gain from his death? What happened to Badger's heart pills? Why does Lily, a former beauty queen, still try to swing her hips—even behind her walker? Buster, a resident and former security guard, and his son, Doyle, a bumbling cop, want to solve this case! *(Requires 15 participants. Includes full, reproducible script, invitation templates, nametags, place settings, and a full set of host/hostess directions. Templates available online for free download.)*

Accuracy
An Interactive Mystery Party Game
for Teens or Adults
S. E. Thomas

A successful, but pompous, author is murdered on the night of his new book debut celebration. A note—intended to stop the murder—actually spurns the killer into action due to some rearranged punctuation. Who wrote the note? Who tampered with the note? Who carried out the false instructions? Nearly everyone has a motive! An intelligent Spanish lawyer with a very thick accent discovers the truth. *(Requires 11 participants. Includes full, reproducible script, invitation templates, nametags, place settings, and a full set of host/hostess directions. Templates available online for free download.)*

Let Them Eat Cake
An Interactive Mystery Party Game for Teens or Adults
S. E. Thomas

A reputable cake-baking contest is underway and the contestants are vying to win 20% of the stock in the wealthy contest sponsor's restaurant business. Then the sponsor turns up dead! He ate an entire cake ridden with arsenic-bearing apple seeds! Who gave him the cake? Who wanted him dead? Why in the world didn't he stop at the first bite? A bumbling security guard who is allergic to flour is on the case! *(Requires 14 participants.)*

A Reason To Celebrate
A Full-Length Christmas Production
S. E. Thomas

For most, Christmas is a time filled with joy. But for many, Christmas can be a difficult season. But let us consider a moment what Scripture tells us of the first Christmas. What really happened? For the first time, God Himself—the Creator of the Universe, the King of Kings, the Everlasting Father—stepped into our world! He stepped in—not to enjoy the wealth or the beauty or the joys—but to experience our suffering, our longings, and our sorrows. From the moment of His birth, He experienced far from ideal circumstances. Yet, we remember His words, "In this world you will have trouble. But take heart! I have overcome the world."

Acting Out Loud
Christian Skits for All Occasions
S. E. Thomas

Whether you are a pastor looking for a skit to help drive home your message, a ministry leader desiring a dramatic reading to speak

God's love at a retreat or conference, or a youth group leader hoping to spice up a youth meeting, we have the material you're looking for! Find over thirty skits, short plays, and dramatic readings that cover the following areas: Biblical Tales, Christian Living, Evangelism, Special Events, Holidays.

Sourdough Secrets… Revealed!
From Making the Starter to Sourdough Success!
Ray Templeton

Step-by-step instructions that will allow you to make your own starter, make your first loaf, and even learn to make sourdough bread in your bread machine.

Is My Faith My Own?
A Resource for Christian Young People Leaving Home for the First Time
S. E. Thomas

Everything was going along fine... then you got out on your own and realized it's your responsibility to get the rest of your life right. From here on out, if you're going to follow God, you're going to be doing it on your own. You can no longer coast by on your parents' faith, your pastor's understanding, or your youth leader's morals. Now it's up to you. And you have some questions: Is my faith real? Is it growing? Is it my own?

Please Visit Us Again!

Find books, study guides, plays, skits, mystery party games, fundraising resources, free downloadable program templates, writers' resources, and much more at:

www.ingramcontent.com/pod-product-compliance
Lightning Source LLC
Chambersburg PA
CBHW031515040426
42445CB00009B/234

* 9 7 8 1 6 4 1 5 7 0 0 9 1 *